Money Sense

Currency

Andrew Einspruch

A+

This edition first published in 2012 in the United States of America by Smart Apple Media.
All rights reserved. No part of this book may be reproduced in any form or by any means
without written permission from the publisher.

Smart Apple Media
P.O. Box 3263
Mankato, MN, 56002

First published in 2011 by
MACMILLAN EDUCATION AUSTRALIA PTY LTD
15–19 Claremont St, South Yarra, Australia 3141

Visit our web site at www.macmillan.com.au or go directly to www.macmillanlibrary.com.au

Associated companies and representatives throughout the world.

Copyright text © Macmillan Publishers Australia 2011

Library of Congress Cataloging-in-Publication Data has been applied for

Publisher: Carmel Heron
Commissioning Editor: Niki Horin
Managing Editor: Vanessa Lanaway
Editors: Tim Clarke and Kirstie Innes-Will
Proofreader: Georgina Garner
Designer (cover and text): Kerri Wilson
Page layout: Kerri Wilson
Photo research: Elizabeth Sim (management: Debbie Gallagher)
Illustrator: Chris Dent
Production Controller: Vanessa Johnson

Manufactured in China by Macmillan Production (Asia) Ltd.
Kwun Tong, Kowloon, Hong Kong
Supplier Code: CP March 2011

Acknowledgments
The author and the publisher are grateful to the following for permission to reproduce copyright material:

Front cover photograph: Corbis/Angelo Cavalli (exchange board); Getty/DAJ, (boy); Shutterstock/Diamond_Images, (background)
/dibrova, (coins), /Bianda Ahmad Hisham, (background).

Back cover photograph: Shutterstock/Diamond_Images, (background), /dibrova (coins), /Bianda Ahmad Hisham, (background).

Gary Ashkenazy, 3 (top), 14 (bottom), 30 (bottom); ©The Trustees of the British Museum. All rights reserved., 12 (foreground), 28
(second row), 31 (bottom); Corbis/Bettmann, 19, 28 (third row), 29, /Angelo Cavalli, 7, /DK Limited/Christopher Cooper, 15, /Somos
Images/Steve Hix, 5; Dreamstime/Eprom, 6 (fourth row, left), /Lawrence Long, 20, /Savageair, 7 (fourth row, left), /Irina Veremeenko,
18 (bottom) Getty/Gary Cook/Visuals Unlimited, Inc., 13 (bottom), /Yadid Levy, 8; GETTY, 11 (top); Reid Goldsworth, 13 (top);
iStockphoto.com/Claudio Divizia, 6 (first row, left), 7 (first row, left), /Philip Dyer, 6 (second row, left), 6 (top), /Tarek El Sombati, 6
(first row, right), /erwo1, 21, /gilaxia, 9, /Sergiy Goruppa, 11 (bottom), /kickers, 12 (background), 29, /Rich Legg, 4, /Maria Toutoudaki,
7 (second row, left), /travellinglight, 7 (fourth row, right); YinYang, 7 (fourth row, right); Pixmac/Jojojojo, 6, (fourth row, right), 32;
Reserve Bank of Australia, 27, 29 (third row); Shutterstock/ARTEKI, 6 (third row, left), /CLM, 10 (bottom), 28 (first row), /Sasha Davas, 7,
(first row, right), /Diamond_Images **throughout** (background), /dibrova, 1, 31 (bottom), /digitalreflections, 26, /Bianda Ahmad Hisham
throughout, (background), /Jan Hopgood, 7 (second row, right), /fstockfoto, 24, /Lipsky, 13, 19 (bottom), 26 (top), /Robyn Mackenzie,
10 (top), 14 (top), 18 (top), /megastocker, 7 (third row, right), /ostromec, 3 (bottom), 6 (second row, right), /sx70, 7 (third row, left);
123RF/Thorsten Rust, 6 (third row, right).

While every care has been taken to trace and acknowledge copyright, the publisher tenders their apologies for any accidental
infringement where copyright has proved untraceable. They would be pleased to come to a suitable arrangement with the rightful
owner in each case.

Please note
At the time of printing, the Internet addresses appearing in this book were correct. Owing to the dynamic nature of the Internet,
however, we cannot guarantee that all these addresses will remain correct.

Contents

Money Sense　4

Currency　5

Major Currencies of the World　6

Before Currency　8

The First Currency　10

Coins　12

How Are Coins Minted?　16

Paper Money　18

How Is Paper Money Printed?　22

Governments and Currency　24

Counterfeit Currency　26

A Timeline of Currency　28

Find Out More　30

Glossary　31

Index　32

Glossary Words

When a word is printed in **bold**, you can look up its meaning in the Glossary on page 31.

Money Sense

Money — it makes sense to know about it. People use money and think about it every day. How much money does this cost? Do I have enough money to buy that? Should I save my money for something? All of the answers to these questions relate to understanding how money works.

Money Matters

Like it or not, money matters. It matters whether people have a lot of money or just a little. How much money people have and how they manage their money both affect the life choices they can make. A decision today, such as saving money or spending it, can affect what they can do months and years from now.

Money is better than poverty, if only for financial reasons.

Woody Allen, film director

Asking yourself "What does money let me do?" can help you develop good money sense.

Currency

Money can be anything that people use to pay for things. However, when people think of money they usually think of a kind of money called currency, which includes only coins and notes. The important thing about currency is not the physical coins and notes, but how they can be used.

How Currency Is Used

Currency is money that is used to buy **goods** and **services**. If a person wants to buy a good, such as food, or a service, such as entry to a movie, then he or she can use currency.

This works because the buyer and the seller agree that the currency they are using has value. A certain amount of currency will transfer ownership of the item or use of the service from one person to another. Currency turns that agreement into something that can be touched.

This girl is exchanging currency in return for a drink.

Major Currencies of the World

Most countries have their own currency. The big exception is most countries in the **European Union**, which use a currency called the euro.

United States
The United States (U.S.) dollar is the most used currency around the world, due to the high level of buying and selling that Americans do.

European Union
The euro is the official currency of the European Union. Many countries in Europe use it. It was first used in 1999, and it is the second most used currency after the U.S. dollar.

China
Renminbi is Chinese for "people's money." The yuan is a unit of money in the Chinese renminbi money system, in the same way that cents and dollars are part of the U.S. money system.

Japan
The Japanese yen is the third most traded currency in the world, after the U.S. dollar and the euro. It was first used in 1869.

Exchange Rates

People cannot use the same currency everywhere. When they go to another country, they usually have to exchange one currency for another. **Exchange rates** tell them how much one country's currency is worth in relation to another country's currency. Exchange rates change daily, depending on many things, such as how the **economy** of the country is performing compared to the economies of other countries.

United Kingdom

The name of the British currency, "pound sterling," comes from around 775 CE, when the Saxons, the people living in Britain at the time, created silver coins known as sterlings. They made 240 of them from 1 pound (454 g) of silver.

Australia

Australia uses dollars. In 1988, Australia became the first country to issue notes made of **polymer** instead of paper.

Canada

Like the U.S., Australia, and Hong Kong, Canada uses the symbol $ to represent its dollar.

New Zealand

Before New Zealand changed its currency to the dollar in 1967, it used pounds and pence. "Kiwi" and "zeal" were also considered as names for the currency.

Before Currency

Before currency was used, what did people do when they wanted goods and services?

Gift Economy

In the past, some societies had what is called a **gift economy**. A gift economy is where people give things to each other without expecting to receive anything in return. If a person has more than enough of everything he or she needs, the person can give some away to make sure someone else has enough.

Bartering

As human societies developed, people started **bartering**. Bartering is trading one kind of good or service for another good or service. If I have carrots and you have shoes, and I want shoes and you want carrots, we can barter. This means coming to an agreement about how many carrots I can exchange for a pair of shoes.

People have come to markets for thousands of years to barter their goods and services. The Grand Bazaar in Istanbul, Turkey, which opened in 1461, is one of the oldest roofed markets still in use.

> The propensity [tendency] to ... barter and exchange one thing for another is common to all men, and is found in no other race of animals.
>
> Adam Smith, Scottish philosopher and economist

The Problem: Matching Wants

Bartering is difficult if the good or service being offered is not valued by the other person. If I want your shoes but you are not interested in my carrots, we can try to find a third person, perhaps someone who has scissors. If you want scissors, I could trade some carrots for scissors, then trade the scissors for your shoes. It gets complicated very quickly!

The Solution: Currency

People began using currency as a way of trading without needing to find something that the other person wanted. By using currency, I can sell my carrots to anyone who wants them. I can then use the currency I receive to buy whatever I want. Problem solved!

Using currency makes the trade of goods and services much simpler than bartering.

The First Currency

People did not move straight from bartering to using currency as we know it today — they used **commodities** as a stepping stone.

What Are Commodities?

The first things that people used as currency were commodities. Commodities are things that people grow or find, and that can be easily traded, such as corn or lumps of gold.

MONEY FACT

People have used many different things as currency throughout history, including gold, silver, copper, salt, peppercorns, large stones, decorated belts, shells, alcohol, cigarettes, and tea.

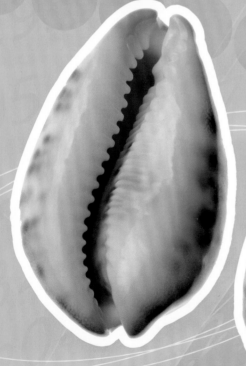

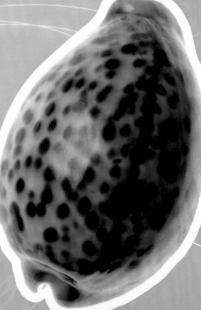

Cowry shells were a commodity used as currency in China 3,000 years ago. Chinese characters to do with money all contain the character for a cowry shell.

Food commodities, such as corn, can spoil, making them worthless as currency.

The Advantages of Using Commodities

The biggest advantage of using commodities as currency is that everyone can agree that the commodity has value. Corn can be eaten and a piece of gold can be used to make something. Another advantage of commodities is that they can be easily divided into smaller amounts. Corn can be divided into bushels and gold can be cut into pieces.

The Disadvantages of Using Commodities

Some commodities, such as foods, can spoil. No one is interested in trading anything of value for an old piece of corn! Also, commodities are not always convenient to carry around. Imagine how hard it would be to carry heavy bags of gold when you wanted to buy something expensive.

Gold is a valuable commodity that is used to make items, such as jewelry.

COINS

Commodities have actual value, but coins represent value. Early coins were made from precious metals, such as gold and silver, which were also considered commodities. However, over time, coins became less about the value of the metal they were made of and more about the value that the coins represented.

Early Coins: Turtles From Aegina

Some of the earliest coins were used on the Greek island of Aegina, around 650 BCE. These coins were made of silver and featured engravings of a turtle on one side and a square divided into parts on the other. The turtle was an appropriate symbol because it represented the Greek goddess Aphrodite and the fact that the Aeginetans were famous seafarers.

These early coins from Aegina in Greece were commonly called "turtles," with a turtle engraved on one side and a pattern on the other.

Why Is Metal Used for Currency?

Unlike commodities such as corn or tea, metal does not spoil. There is a lot of metal around, and it is easy to work with. Metal can also be recycled by melting it down again.

> For things to have value in man's world, they are given the role of commodities.
>
> Ana Castillo, U.S. writer

Early coins from Lydia featured a lion's head, which was the symbol of the king.

Early Coins: Lydian Lions

Around the same time, the Lydians, in what is now Turkey, also used coins. In Lydia there was a lot of electrum, which is a natural mix of silver and gold. However, electrum was not as valuable as either pure gold or pure silver, so the Lydians melted it down into circles to make coins.

The Spread of Coins

After coins were introduced, more and more people around the world realized that coins were an easy and convenient way of conducting trade. Within a few hundred years, coins were being used across Europe and the Middle East.

Coins often had an animal on them or an image associated with the place they were from. Later it became popular to have a symbol of the city on one side and the head of a god or goddess on the other.

MONEY FACT

Gold is valuable because it is hard to find, dense, and easy to store. All of these features make it good for use as currency.

Like the Greeks, the Chinese were early users of coins. This bronze coin comes from the Han Dynasty, around 100 BCE.

Standard Size and Weight

For coins to be used as currency, people needed to be happy that one coin was just like any other. Coins were therefore made to a standard size and weight.

Purity

Coins also had to be of a certain purity, which is a measure of the amount of metal in the coin compared to other substances. Small slabs of dark stone, called touchstones, were used to test the purity of soft metals such as gold. When a soft metal is rubbed on a touchstone, it leaves a visible line. The color of the line tells a person how pure the soft metal is. This test helped people create coins with reliably pure content.

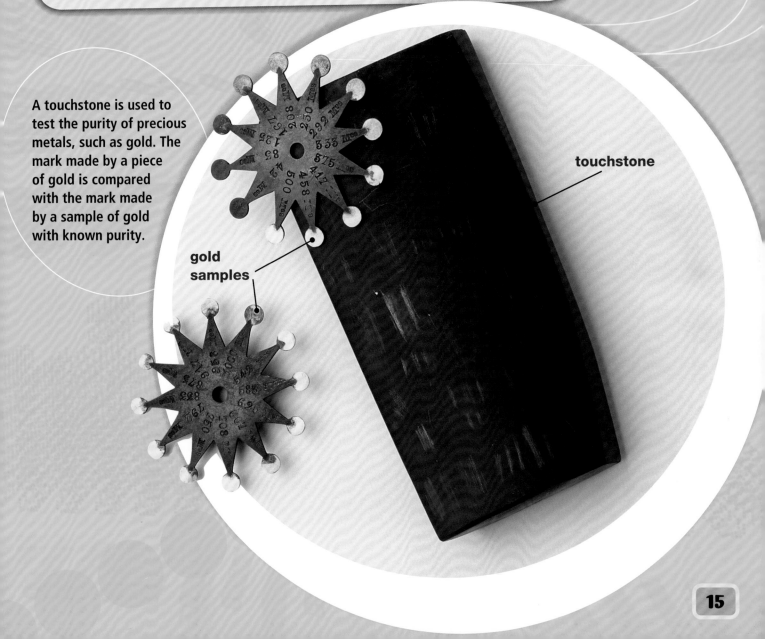

A touchstone is used to test the purity of precious metals, such as gold. The mark made by a piece of gold is compared with the mark made by a sample of gold with known purity.

gold samples

touchstone

How Are Coins Minted?

Every year, billions of coins are produced around the world. Each coin is designed and manufactured in a special factory called a **mint**. The process of manufacturing coins is called minting.

1 Designing a Coin

1. A designer creates a design for the coin. The coin may have a new design on one or both sides.

2. The design is approved by the government.

3. A sculptor creates a model of the coin in clay. Plaster is poured on the clay model.
   OR
   Computer software is used to create a digital model of the coin.

4. The final design is checked for any mistakes, such as letters in the wrong place or missing parts of the design.

5. Computer software is used to translate the design into the instructions needed to make a **die**, which is a tool used to stamp the design into the metal of the coin. Each coin needs two die, one for the top (head) and one for the bottom (tail).

6. A machine cuts the coin design into a smooth, blank piece of steel.

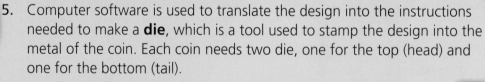

7. The piece of steel is used to create a die. The die is used to stamp the coins.

2 Making the Blank Coins

1. The metals used in the coins are mixed together and rolled into long sheets that are about 12 inches (30 cm) wide, 1,500 feet (450 m) long, and up to 6,000 pounds (2,700 kg).

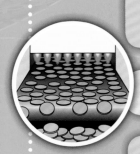

2. Discs called blanks are cut from the sheets. They are a bit bigger than the actual coins, but weigh the same as finished coins.

3. The blanks are heated, which softens the metal.

4. The softened blanks are washed and dried. The discs are now called **planchets**.

5. A rim is raised on the edge of the planchets, making them the size of the finished coin. The rim goes over both edges of the coin and is higher than the highest point of the finished coin, which protects the coin.

3 Minting the Coins

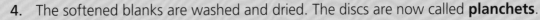

1. The planchets are fed into a stamping press, where they are held in a coin collar.

2. The tails die stays still, while the heads die moves. It acts as a hammer to stamp the design of the coin into the planchet. The amount of force and time needed depends on the metal used in the coin. Fast presses can stamp hundreds of coins each minute.

3. The coins go into a collection box and then onto a conveyor belt.

4. The coins are inspected and any that have errors are recycled.

5. The coins are counted, bagged, and then delivered to **banks**.

Paper Money

Paper money, or banknotes, evolved as an alternative currency to coins. Paper money became a popular currency around 1,200 years after the first coins were used.

Paper Money Versus Coins

Coins came before paper money and have several advantages. Because they are made of metal, they last longer. They are harder to **counterfeit**. Also, they have more actual value than paper money because of the metal they contain.

However, paper money has several advantages over coins. Paper money is cheaper to make because paper is cheaper than metal. Paper money is also more convenient to carry around than coins, which can be heavy in large amounts.

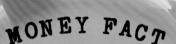

MONEY FACT
If you stacked $1,000,000 in $1 bills, the stack would be more than 358 feet (109 m) tall!

Paper money makes it easier to carry more currency.

The First Paper Money

Paper money first became popular in China sometime after 600 CE. If you were rich and had lots of coins, they were hard to carry around. These coins could be left with someone you trusted. In return, that person gave you a paper note saying how much you had left with him or her. If you brought the note back to the person, he or she would give back the amount you had left. Over time, people started trading the notes themselves.

The oldest known paper money, now kept in a museum, was first used in China more than 1,000 years ago.

Early Chinese Notes

Around 960 CE, China found it did not have much copper available for making coins. So it started using notes, called *jiaozi*. This became the world's first widely used paper money.

Early Paper Money

Early paper money is sometimes called representative money, because the paper note represented the value of something else, such as coins or precious metal. If you had the paper note and requested what it represented, the issuer of the note had to give it to you.

Banknotes

At first, almost anyone could issue paper money. However, paper money was only as reliable as the person or business who issued it. If you had a note from a trader that went out of business, the note became worthless. Therefore, only paper money from the largest and most trusted institutions, such as banks, became widely used. This is how paper money evolved into banknotes.

SILVER CERTIFICATE

...RTIFIES THAT THERE IS ON DEPOSIT IN THE TREASU...

...ITED STATES OF A...

This U.S. silver certificate is an example of representative money. People could present it and demand the same amount in silver dollar coins.

Governments Issue Currency

Over time, most governments decided that they should be the only ones able to issue currency. People trusted a country's currency more when it was backed by the government.

Once governments were in charge, paper money did not always represent an amount of precious metals. During times of national stress, such as wars, there might not be enough precious metals to back up the paper money that governments had issued.

Value by Fiat

Rather than representing an amount of precious metals, money from the government was given value by **fiat**. Fiat is a Latin word that means "let it be done." By using a fiat, the government said, "This is our country's money. Everyone has to use it." Because people believe that the government will back up their country's currency, they trust it and use it.

Today, currencies such as these Swiss francs are given value by government fiat.

How Is Paper Money Printed?

Governments produce a steady supply of paper money every year. Paper money is printed under strictly controlled conditions. The following steps show how some paper money is printed.

1 Design and Preparation of Paper Money

1. Designers create a design for paper money using computer software or by drawing it by hand.

2. Engravers cut the design into a metal plate. This is called the master die.

3. The master die is inspected and approved by the government.

4. Thin plastic is pressed into the master die to create a raised version of the design. Then 32 layers of these plastic impressions are joined together in a pattern that consists of 4 impressions across and 8 impressions down, which amounts to 32 bills.

5. The plastic impressions are covered in copper. The plastic is then taken away, leaving a raised impression of the design. It is cleaned, polished, inspected, and approved. Then it is covered in a chemical called chromium. This becomes the master printing plate.

2 The Materials

1. The paper used for paper money is a special blend, which varies between countries. In Australia, polymer is used. In the U.S., the paper is 75 percent cotton and 25 percent linen. The paper is made in a carefully controlled way that is hard to copy.

2. Modern paper money is more colorful than older paper money. These colors make modern paper money harder to counterfeit. The printing is done carefully so the detailed designs of the paper notes come out clearly.

3 Manufacture

1. First, 10,000 sheets of paper are loaded into a printing press. This will produce 320,000 notes.

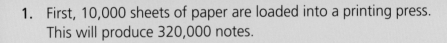

2. The master printing plate is covered in ink and excess ink is removed.

3. The sheets of paper are fed into the printing press and printed with ink.

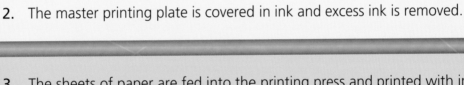

4. The sheets dry for a day or two, then the other side is printed.

5. The printed stacks are cut into two pieces, giving two stacks of 10,000 sheets, with 16 notes on each.

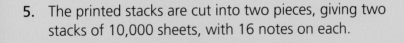

6. The finished sheets are inspected for mistakes.

7. The sheets are divided into stacks of 100 sheets, which are then cut into individual notes.

8. The paper money is wrapped and prepared for delivery to banks.

Governments and Currency

Around the world, governments are in charge of their countries' currency. People trust their currency because their government stands behind it.

Central Banks

The part of a government that is in charge of a country's currency is called the **central bank**. The central bank has different names in different countries, such as the Federal Reserve in the U.S., the European Central Bank in Europe, the Reserve Bank in Australia and New Zealand, and the Bank of Canada in Canada.

What Do Central Banks Do?

A country's central bank does many important things, such as:

- it decides how much money should be created for people to use (the money supply)
- it creates the notes and coins (currency) and issues them
- it sets **interest rates**, which affect how much it costs to borrow money
- it acts as a banker for the government
- it oversees the country's banking system

The Federal Reserve is the central bank for the U.S. Its main building is in Washington, D.C.

Monetary Policy

Deciding on monetary policy is the central bank's main job. This involves issuing currency, managing the money supply, and changing the cost of borrowing money. The central bank's overall goal is to keep the country's currency stable over time.

Inflation

If currency is unstable, **inflation** occurs. If the price of something increases from $1 to $1.10, more money is needed to buy the same thing. This also means that the currency is worth less. The central bank tries to control inflation so that the country's currency is worth almost the same amount over time.

Companies advertise the fact that prices rise over time to try and persuade people to buy their products sooner rather than later.

SAVE ON MP3 PLAYERS

DIGITAL TV SPECIAL

BUY NOW AND BEAT THE PRICE RISE

The **mint** makes it first, it is up to you to make it last.

Evan Esar, U.S. writer

Counterfeit Currency

Counterfeit currency is fake money that is used as though it is real. Counterfeiters usually try to make fake paper money rather than coins, as it is usually too expensive to counterfeit coins.

Why Is Counterfeit Money a Problem?

If people could print their own currency, they could have as much as they wanted. However, money is an agreement. People agree that the money they use has value. If anyone could print money, people would no longer trust the money or agree that it had value. That is why only the government is allowed to create money.

Early Counterfeiting

Counterfeiting started around the same time that currency started to be used. For example, currency was used in Ancient Rome, and counterfeit Roman currency has been found.

These counterfeit banknotes look very similar to real banknotes.

Fighting Counterfeiters

There are lots of different ways to make it hard to counterfeit paper money, such as:

- including lots of details in the design
- using a printing process called intaglio, which creates raised printing
- including three-dimensional pictures called holograms
- using many different colored inks
- using microprinting, which means including very small text that is not easily seen by the naked eye
- using inks that change color depending on the angle of light
- printing the notes on a polymer that is hard to get or match

These different techniques make it too difficult and expensive to produce convincing paper money.

microprinting

Australian banknotes have many features that make them difficult to counterfeit.

polymer instead of paper

detailed design

multiple colors

A Timeline of Currency

1200 BCE

Cowry shells are used as money in China.

Around 650 BCE

Coins are first used in Aegina (Greece) and in Lydia (Turkey).

960 CE

Paper notes are issued in China, as there is a shortage of the copper needed for making coins.

1275–1292

European explorer Marco Polo visits China, where he learns about paper money. He brings this idea back to Europe.

1294

Paper money is printed in Persia (now Iran).

1344

In England, the weight of a penny is lessened, which is the first change in its currency in more than 200 years.

Around 1455

China stops using paper money. Their money system becomes based on silver.

1764

Britain tells its American colonies that they cannot issue their own paper money.

1778

Oliver Pollock, a New Orleans businessman, creates the dollar symbol ($).

1789

The new Constitution of the U.S. gives the Federal Government the power to issue money. Individual states cannot issue their own notes or coins.

1797

The Bank of England issues the very first £1 note.

1816

Gold is officially made the standard for value in England.

1935

China's central bank begins using a fiat currency.

1944–1946

There is terrible inflation in Europe, and in some countries, such as Hungary, money becomes worthless.

1966

The first cash dispensing machine is used in Tokyo, Japan, with other countries following soon after.

1988

Australia issues the first banknotes made of polymer instead of paper.

2002

Euro notes and coins are used in the European Union for the first time.

2003

The US introduces a new $20 note that is harder to counterfeit.

2011

The euro replaces the kroon as the official currency of Estonia.

Find Out More

Improve your money sense by finding out more about the history of currency and how it is used around the world.

Web Sites

http://en.wikipedia.org

Wikipedia has a number of articles about currency.
Try searching for "coins," "banknotes," and "history of money,"

www.howstuffworks.com

The How Stuff Works web site has articles on how coins are made and how banknotes are printed. Search for "how currency works."

www.newmoney.gov

This web site has a lot of information about the new $100 United States banknote, which started circulating in 2011.

www.xe.com

This web site shows what today's foreign exchange rates are and calculates amounts for many different currencies.

Places to Visit

Mints

Many cities have mints where money is printed. Most of these allow people to tour them to see the process of making coins or paper money.

Central Banks

Central banks often have museums dedicated to money. For example:

- the Museum of Australian Currency, located in the Reserve Bank Building in Sydney, tells the story of Australia's currency as it developed along with the country's history
- the Federal Reserve Banks of Chicago and Kansas City have money museums with lots of interesting historical information about money
- the Bank of Canada in Ottawa has a currency museum with more than 100,000 objects related to the history of money.

Glossary

banks
businesses that hold and lend money
for people

bartering
exchanging goods and services directly,
without using money

BCE
Before the Common Era; before the last
2,000 or so years

CE
Common Era; within the last 2,000 or so years

central bank
the part of a government that is in charge of
a country's currency

commodities
things that are grown or found that can be
easily traded because they are seen as useful
or valuable, such as corn or gold

counterfeit
make fake versions of

die
a tool used to stamp an impression onto a
coin or banknote

economy
all the buying and selling of goods and
services that takes place in a particular place

European Union
an organization set up to promote close
economic and political ties between countries
in Europe

exchange rates
the amounts that different currencies are
worth compared to the currencies of
other countries

fiat
legal decree or command

gift economy
an economy where things are given without
the expectation of getting anything back

goods
things that people can buy and touch

inflation
rising prices, causing money to be
worth less

interest rates
the percentages paid on amounts of
money that are borrowed or deposited

mint
a place where coins are made

planchets
flat, round pieces of metal that get stamped
to make coins

polymer
a kind of plastic used to make banknotes

services
things that people do for other people

Index

A

Aegina (Greece)   12, 28

B

banknotes   18, 20, 26, 27, 29, 30
bartering   8, 9, 10

C

central banks   24, 25, 29, 30
Chinese money   6, 10, 14, 19, 28, 29
coins   5, 7, 12–15, 16–17, 18, 19, 20, 24, 26, 28, 29, 30
commodities   10, 11, 12, 13
counterfeit money   18, 26–27
cowry shells   10, 28
currencies of the world   6–7

D

dies   16, 17, 22
dollar   6, 7, 18, 20

E

euro   6, 29
exchange rates   7, 30

F

Federal Reserve   24, 30
fiats   21, 29

G

gift economy   8
gold   10, 11, 12, 13, 14, 15, 29
governments   16, 21, 22, 24–25, 26, 28

I

inflation   25, 29
interest rates   24

J

jiaozi   19

L

Lydia (Turkey)   13, 28

M

metal   12, 13, 15, 17, 18, 21, 22
minting coins   16–17
mints   16, 25, 30
monetary policy   25
money sense   4

P

paper money   18–21, 22–23, 26, 27, 28, 29, 30
peso   7
planchets   17
polymer   23, 27, 29
pound sterling   7
printing paper money   22–23
purity of coins   15

R

renminbi   6
representative money   20

T

touchstone   15

Y

yen   6